¡Ven conmigo!

Holt Spanish Level 1

Assessment Guide

HOLT, RINEHART AND WINSTON
Harcourt Brace & Company

Austin • New York • Orlando • Atlanta • San Francisco • Boston • Dallas • Toronto • London

Copyright © 1996 by Holt, Rinehart and Winston, Inc.

All rights reserved. No part of this publication may be reproduced or transmitted in any form or by any means, electronic or mechanical, including photocopy, recording, or any information storage and retrieval system, without permission in writing from the publisher.

Permission is hereby granted to reproduce the Black Line Masters in this publication in complete pages for instructional use and not for resale by any teacher using HOLT SPANISH.

Some material appears in this book from other HRW publications.

Printed in the United States of America

ISBN 0-03-094953-X

6 7 8 9   021   99 98

Contents

Portfolio Assessment

To the Teacher 2

Evaluating Written Activities: Form A.. 5

Evaluating Written Activities: Form B.. 6

Evaluating Oral Activities: Form A 7

Evaluating Oral Activities: Form B 8

Documentation of Group Work... 9

Student's Portfolio Checklist 10

Teacher's Portfolio Checklist 11

Portfolio Self-Evaluation 12

Portfolio Evaluation... 13

Portfolio Suggestions: Chapters 1-12.. 14

Speaking Tests

To the Teacher.. 26

Speaking Test Evaluation Form 27

Speaking Tests: Chapters 1-12 28

Midterm and Final Examinations

Midterm Exam 35

    Score Sheet 43

    Listening Scripts.. 46

    Answers 48

Final Exam 49

    Score Sheet 57

    Listening Scripts.. 60

    Answers 62

¡Ven conmigo! Level 1

To the Teacher

Portfolio Assessment

A portfolio is a compilation of work representing a student's ideas, interests, skills, and accomplishments. It can be as basic as a folder assigned by the teacher or as individual as a cardboard box decorated by the student. A portfolio may be a collection of selected pieces, a showcase of samples of a student's best work, or even a high-tech compilation of images showing the student's progress and accomplishments on a videocassette. Student portfolios are of great benefit to foreign language students and teachers alike because they provide documentation of a student's efforts, progress, and achievements over a given period of time. In addition, sharing their portfolio of achievements with the teacher, family, and peers can provide students very positive feedback and be an affirming experience. The opportunity for self-reflection provided by portfolio assessment encourages students to take charge of their learning, fostering pride, ownership, and self-esteem.

This *Assessment Guide* includes a variety of materials that will help you implement portfolios in your classroom. The written and oral activity evaluation forms, student and teacher checklists, portfolio evaluation sheets, and written and oral portfolio suggestions included here are appropriate for use with student portfolios, or they may be used independently as part of any assessment program.

DETERMINING A PURPOSE

The first step in implementing the use of portfolios in your classroom is determining the purpose for which they will be used. You can use portfolios to assess individual students' growth and progress, to make students active in the assessment process, to provide evidence and documentation of students' work for more effective communication with parents, or to evaluate an instructional program or curriculum. Both the contents of the portfolio and the manner in which it is to be evaluated will depend directly on the purpose(s) the portfolio is to serve. Before including any work in their portfolios, students must know the purpose of the portfolio and the criteria by which their work will be evaluated.

SETTING UP THE PORTFOLIOS

While portfolios can be used to meet a variety of objectives, they are especially useful tools for assessing written and oral work in your foreign language classroom. Written items can be in a variety of formats including lists, posters, personal correspondence, poems, stories, articles, and essays, depending on the level and needs of the students. Oral items, such as conversations, interviews, commercials, and skits, should be recorded on audio- or videocassette for incorporation into the portfolio. Whatever the format, both written and oral work should include evidence of the developmental process such as notes from brainstorming, outlines, early drafts, or scripts, as well as the finished product.

Each student will need a container in which to keep the materials selected for his or her portfolio. This could be anything from a basic folder to a cereal box, and many students enjoy personalizing the container of their choice. Remind students that their portfolios will need to accommodate audio or videocassettes as well as papers.

SELECTING MATERIALS FOR THE PORTFOLIO

The ¡Ven conmigo! program is designed to allow flexibility in creating, maintaining, and evaluating student portfolios. Specific portfolio suggestions are provided for each chapter, one written and one oral. In addition, many other activities in the *Pupil's Edition,* the *Annotated Teachers' Edition*, and the *Chapter Resource Books,* as well as an unlimited number of activities you can create yourself, may also be adapted for portfolios.

There are several ways you and your students can go about selecting materials to include in portfolios. The portfolio should not be seen as a repository for all student work; work should be selected on the basis of the portfolio's purpose and the evaluation criteria to be used.

Student Selection Many teachers prefer to let students choose samples of their best work to include in their portfolios. Early in the year, the teacher tells students how many written and oral items to include in their portfolios (for example, one written item and one oral item per chapter) but allows the students the freedom to choose those pieces that they feel best represent their ability in the language. In this case, the written and oral portfolio items suggested in the *Assessment Guide* would be treated as any other writing or speaking activities, and students would have the option of whether or not to include these in their portfolios. The advantage of this type of portfolio is that it empowers students by placing the decisions about what to include in their hands. Their feeling of ownership of the portfolio will increase as their involvement at the decision-making level increases.

Teacher-Directed Selection Some teachers prefer to maintain portfolios that contain students' responses to specific prompts or activities. The oral and written portfolio items suggested in the *Assessment Guide*, or other writing and speaking activities of the teacher's choice, could be assigned specifically for inclusion in the portfolio. This type of portfolio allows the teacher to focus attention on specific functions, vocabulary items, and grammar points.

Collaborative Selection A third option is some combination of the two approaches described above. The teacher can assign specific activities from which students may choose what to include in their portfolios, or the teacher can assign some specific activities and allow the students to choose others on their own. The collaborative approach allows the teacher to focus on specific objectives while at the same time giving students the opportunity to showcase their best work.

As the classroom teacher, you are in the best position to decide what type of portfolio is most beneficial for your program and students. The most important step is to decide along with your students what objectives and outcomes the portfolio should assess and then assign or help students select items that will best reflect those objectives and outcomes.

USING THE PORTFOLIO CHECKLISTS

Regardless of the method of material selection you choose, the checklists on pages 10 and 11 will help you and your students keep the portfolios organized. The *Student's Portfolio Checklist* is designed to help students track the items they include. The *Teacher's Portfolio Checklist* is a running list of the items you expect students to include. If you choose to allow students to select materials for their portfolios, the teacher's list will be very general, specifying only the types of items and the dates on which each should be included. Your checklist will be more specific if you are assigning specific portfolio activities, as it should indicate the particular activities you have assigned and the dates on which they are to be included.

EVALUATING THE PORTFOLIO

Evaluating Individual Items The *Assessment Guide* provides a variety of forms that will help you and your students evaluate the portfolios. The written and oral activity evaluation forms, *Evaluating Written Activities* and *Evaluating Oral Activities,* found on pages 5–8 are designed to help you and your students evaluate individual speaking and writing activities. These forms can be used by the teacher or by the students for peer- or self-evaluation. The written and oral evaluation forms labeled **A** provide a holistic assessment, while the forms labeled **B** provide a more quantitative or analytic assessment. Use of these forms gives students helpful feedback and helps keep them on the right track throughout the assessment period.

Documenting Group Work Very often a group-work project cannot be included in an individual's portfolio because of its size or the difficulties involved in making copies for each group member (posters, bulletin boards, videos, etc.). Other group or pair activities, such as conversations or skits, cannot be included in the portfolio unless they are recorded. To help students document such activities in their portfolios, you may want to use the form *Documentation of Group Work* on page 9.

Evaluating the Total Portfolio Exactly how and how often you evaluate your students' total portfolios will depend on the stated purpose. Ideally, students' portfolios should be evaluated at regular intervals over the course of the academic year. You should establish the length of the assessment period in advance—six weeks, a quarter, a semester, etc. The *Portfolio Self-Evaluation* and *Portfolio Evaluation* forms on pages 12–13 are designed to aid you and your students in assessing the portfolio at the end of each assessment period. In order to ensure that portfolios are progressing successfully, you will want to meet individually with each student throughout each assessment period. In addition, individual conferences with students should be scheduled at the end of each evaluation period to discuss their portfolios and compare your assessment with their own.

Nombre _____ Clase _____ Fecha _____

Evaluating Written Activities

Form A   Item _____   Chapter _____

OVERALL IMPRESSION

☐ Excellent   ☐ Good   ☐ Satisfactory   ☐ Unsatisfactory

Some aspects of this item that are particularly good are _____
_____
_____
_____
_____

Some areas that could be improved are _____
_____
_____
_____
_____

To improve your written work, I recommend _____
_____
_____
_____
_____

Additional Comments:
_____
_____
_____
_____

¡Ven conmigo! Level 1

Nombre _____ Clase _____ Fecha _____

Evaluating Written Activities

Form B   Item _____   Chapter _____

CONTENT
4 Complete. The writer has clearly conveyed the main idea and has provided supporting details that are relevant and interesting.
3 Generally complete. The writer has conveyed the main idea, but has not given adequate relevant details to support it.
2 Incomplete. The main idea is unclear. Much of the detail is irrelevant.
1 Incomplete. The main idea is unclear. Details are nonexistent or random and irrelevant.

COMPREHENSIBILITY
4 Very comprehensible. The student uses appropriate language to convey the main idea clearly.
3 Comprehensible. The message in this item is unclear in places. The language used is inadequate to make the message totally clear.
2 Somewhat incomprehensible. The message could only be understood by a sympathetic native speaker. The language used is often inappropriate or distorted by interference from English.
1 Incomprehensible.

ORGANIZATION AND PRESENTATION
4 Well organized and presented in an appropriate format. The order is logical and effective, and sequencing words are used consistently and appropriately. The presentation helps communicate the main idea.
3 Generally well organized with a few minor problems. The writer uses adequate sequencing words with few mistakes.
2 Poorly organized. Order is illogical and confusing in places. Sequencing words are used inappropriately or incorrectly. The presentation of this item detracts from the main idea.
1 Presentation is inappropriate. The lack of organization distorts or completely obscures the main idea.

ACCURACY
4 Functions, grammar, and vocabulary are used correctly. Spelling, capitalization, and punctuation are generally correct.
3 Any mistakes in usage are minor and do not distort meaning or inhibit communication. Spelling, capitalization, and punctuation mistakes are infrequent.
2 Problems in usage significantly distort meaning and inhibit communication in some instances. Frequent mistakes in spelling, capitalization, and punctuation disrupt the flow.
1 Problems in usage distort meaning and completely inhibit communication. Mistakes in spelling, capitalization, and punctuation make the item incomprehensible.

EFFORT
4 Exceeds the minimum requirements of the assignment and provides evidence of thoughtful input.
3 Fulfills the minimum requirements of the assignment and provides evidence of thoughtful input.
2 Fulfills the minimum requirements of the assignment but does not show evidence of thoughtful input.
1 Does not fulfill the minimum requirements of the assignment or provide evidence of thoughtful input.

☐ **Total points**

18–20: Excellent
14–17: Good
10–13: Satisfactory
 5–9: Unsatisfactory

COMMENTS:

Nombre _____ Clase _____ Fecha _____

Evaluating Oral Activities

Form A   Item _____   Chapter _____

OVERALL IMPRESSION
☐ Excellent   ☐ Good   ☐ Satisfactory   ☐ Unsatisfactory

Some aspects of this item that are particularly good are _____
_____
_____
_____
_____

Some areas that could be improved are _____
_____
_____
_____
_____

To improve your speaking, I recommend _____
_____
_____
_____
_____

Additional Comments:
_____
_____
_____
_____

¡Ven conmigo! Level 1   Assessment Guide **7**

HRW material copyrighted under notice appearing earlier in this work.

Nombre _____ Clase _____ Fecha _____

Evaluating Oral Activities

Form B Item _____ Chapter _____

CONTENT
4 Complete. The speaker clearly conveys the main idea and provides details that are relevant and interesting.
3 Generally complete. The speaker conveys the main idea, but does not provide adequate relevant details to support it.
2 Somewhat incomplete. The main idea is unclear. Much of the detail is irrelevant.
1 Incomplete. The main idea is unclear. Details are nonexistent or random and irrelevant.

COMPREHENSIBILITY
4 Comprehensible. The speaker uses appropriate language to convey the main idea of this item clearly.
3 Comprehensible. The message is unclear in places. The language used is inadequate to make the message totally clear.
2 Somewhat incomprehensible. The message could only be understood by a sympathetic native speaker. The language used is often inappropriate or distorted by interference from English.
1 Incomprehensible.

FLUENCY
4 The student speaks very clearly without hesitation. Pronunciation and intonation sound natural.
3 The student speaks with some hesitation. Problems with pronunciation and intonation do not prevent communication.
2 The student hesitates frequently. Problems with pronunciation and intonation distort meaning and inhibit communication in some instances.
1 Frequent hesitations and extreme problems with pronunciation cause communication to break down.

ACCURACY
4 Functions, grammar, and vocabulary are used correctly.
3 Minor problems in usage do not distort meaning or inhibit communication.
2 Problems in usage significantly distort meaning and inhibit communication in some instances.
1 Problems in usage completely distort meaning and inhibit communication.

EFFORT
4 Exceeds the minimum requirements of the assignment and provides evidence of thoughtful input.
3 Fulfills the minimum requirements of the assignment and provides evidence of thoughtful input.
2 Fulfills the minimum requirements of the assignment but does not show evidence of thoughtful input.
1 Does not fulfill the minimum requirements of the assignment or provide evidence of thoughtful input.

☐ Total points

18–20: Excellent
14–17: Good
10–13: Satisfactory
 5–9: Unsatisfactory

COMMENTS:
_____
_____
_____
_____
_____
_____
_____

Nombre _____ Clase _____ Fecha _____

Documentation of Group Work

Item _____ Chapter _____

Group Members: _____
_____
_____
_____
_____
_____

Description of Item: _____
_____
_____
_____
_____
_____
_____

Personal Contribution: _____
_____
_____
_____
_____
_____
_____
_____

Please rate your personal contribution to the group's work.

☐ Excellent ☐ Good ☐ Satisfactory ☐ Unsatisfactory

¡Ven conmigo! Level 1

Nombre _____ Clase _____ Fecha _____

 Student's Portfolio Checklist

To the Student This form should be used to keep track of the materials you are including in your portfolio. It is important that you keep this list up to date so that your portfolio will be complete at the end of the assessment period. As you build your portfolio, try to include pieces of your work that demonstrate progress in your ability to speak and write in Spanish.

	Type of Item	Date Completed	Date Placed in Portfolio
Item #1			
Item #2			
Item #3			
Item #4			
Item #5			
Item #6			
Item #7			
Item #8			
Item #9			
Item #10			
Item #11			
Item #12			

Nombre _____ Clase _____ Fecha _____

Teacher's Portfolio Checklist

To the Teacher This form should be used to keep track of the materials you expect your students to keep in their portfolios for the semester. Encourage students to keep their lists up to date so that their portfolios will be complete at the end of the assessment period.

	Type of Item	Date Assigned	Date Due in Portfolio
Item #1			
Item #2			
Item #3			
Item #4			
Item #5			
Item #6			
Item #7			
Item #8			
Item #9			
Item #10			
Item #11			
Item #12			

¡Ven conmigo! Level 1

Nombre _____ Clase _____ Fecha _____

Portfolio Self-Evaluation

To the Student Your portfolio consists of selections of your written and oral work. You should consider all the items in your portfolio as you evaluate your progress. Read the statements below and mark the box to the right of each statement that shows how well your portfolio demonstrates your skills and abilities in Spanish.

	Strongly Agree	Agree	Disagree	Strongly Disagree
1. My portfolio contains all of the required items.				
2. My portfolio provides evidence of my progress in speaking and writing Spanish.				
3. The items in my portfolio demonstrate that I can communicate my ideas in Spanish.				
4. The items in my portfolio demonstrate accurate use of Spanish.				
5. The items in my portfolio show that I understand and can use a wide variety of vocabulary.				
6. When creating the items in my portfolio, I tried to use what I have learned in new ways.				
7. The items in my portfolio provide an accurate picture of my skills and abilities in Spanish.				

My favorite item in my portfolio is _____

because (please give at least three reasons) _____

_____

_____

_____

_____

_____

_____

In assessing my overall portfolio, I find it to be (check one):

☐ Excellent   ☐ Good   ☐ Satisfactory   ☐ Unsatisfactory

Nombre _____ Clase _____ Fecha _____

 Portfolio Evaluation

To the Student I have reviewed the items in your portfolio and want to share with you my reactions to your work.

Teacher's Signature _____

Date _____

	Strongly Agree	Agree	Disagree	Strongly Disagree
1. Your portfolio contains all of the required items.				
2. Your portfolio provides evidence of your progress in speaking and writing Spanish.				
3. The items in your portfolio demonstrate that you can communicate your ideas in Spanish.				
4. The items in your portfolio demonstrate accurate use of Spanish.				
5. The items in your portfolio demonstrate the use of a wide variety of Spanish vocabulary.				
6. When creating the items in your portfolio, you have tried to use what you have learned in new ways.				
7. The items in your portfolio provide an accurate picture of your skills and abilities in Spanish.				

My favorite item in your portfolio is _____

because _____

_____

_____

One area in which you seem to need improvement is _____

_____

For your next portfolio collection, I would like to suggest _____

_____

In assessing your overall portfolio, I find it to be (check one):

☐ Excellent   ☐ Good   ☐ Satisfactory   ☐ Unsatisfactory

CAPÍTULO 1: ¡Mucho gusto!

Portfolio Suggestions

Written: Activity 36, p. 35, *Pupil's Edition*

Expanded Activity Students should imagine that they have met several Spanish-speaking exchange students who don't know English very well yet. They want to make a good impression and introduce their Spanish-speaking friends to the teacher in Spanish, telling their names, ages, and hometowns. Instruct students to write the necessary questions on an index card to get this information. They should then interview the other students and write the answers on their index cards.

Purpose To practice writing simple questions and answers in Spanish. The targeted functions are introducing people and responding to an introduction, asking and saying how old someone is, and asking where someone is from.

Rationale Applying the targeted functional expressions to an authentic situation helps students recognize that they're learning language for communication. Writing these expressions in an authentic context also helps students to internalize the expressions.

Materials Each student will need a 3 x 5 inch index card and a pen.

Portfolio Item Students should put the index cards with interview questions and answers into their portfolios. Taping the index cards to an 8 1/2 x 11 inch piece of paper may make storage easier.

Oral: Repaso Activity 5, p. 39, *Pupil's Edition*

Expanded Activity Students will use the information they got in their interviews to make introductions at a party. Be sure students have memorized the information written on their cards, because they should not use the cards during the role-play. Move the classroom furniture to create a party area by arranging chairs around an empty space. Use the door of the classroom as the front door of the teacher's apartment. Some students are already at the party, and others are in the hall ready to arrive. Arriving at the party, the students exchange greetings and introduce the newcomers to their friends and to the teacher, telling each person's name, age, and hometown.

Purpose To practice making introductions. The targeted functions are saying hello and goodbye, introducing people and responding to an introduction, asking and saying how old someone is, asking where someone is from and saying where you're from.

Rationale Simulating real situations helps students activate the language, thus accelerating their learning.

Materials You will need audio or video equipment to record the activity and individual cassettes or a class master for incorporation into students' portfolios.

Portfolio Item Record students' greetings and introductions on audio- or videocassette for incorporation into their portfolios.

¡Organízate!

Portfolio Suggestions

Written: Activity 2, p. 62, *Pupil's Edition*

Expanded Activity Have each student bring a photo of two or more people they know to class and use it as a centerpiece around which to write sentences. They should tell who each person is, the person's age, and something he or she needs or wants for school or for his or her room at home. The finished product can be mounted on poster board or construction paper and posted in the classroom.

Purpose To practice talking about what people need and want and to review skills learned in **Capítulo 1**. The targeted functions are introducing someone, saying how old someone is, talking about likes and dislikes, and talking about what someone wants and needs.

Rationale Talking about people they know captures the students' interest. Writing something that everyone can read and discuss gives students another opportunity to use the new language and practice their newly acquired vocabulary.

Materials Pen/pencil and paper; poster board or construction paper, glue stick.

Portfolio Item Either the finished product or a photocopy of it can be placed in the student's portfolio.

Oral: A ver si puedo... Activity 2, p. 64, *Pupil's Edition*

Expanded Activity Have students work with partners. Each pair creates a description of an ideal bedroom. Have them discuss together what things they want or need in the room. What do they NOT want or need? Are there things they agree on? When students have finished their description, record their conversation on video or audio tape.

Purpose To practice describing the contents of one's room; to practice telling what you want or need; to practice listening and responding to a partner.

Rationale Knowing the vocabulary and structures necessary to discuss one's personal space allows students to talk about something that is important to them.

Materials Audio or video recording equipment.

Portfolio Item Recording of the conversation.

Nuevas clases, nuevos amigos

Portfolio Suggestions

Written: Repaso Activity 2, p. 92, *Pupil's Edition*

Expanded Activity Each student writes his or her class schedule, using a form, either written on the board or as a handout. The form should look like the class schedule on p. 92 and should include times, courses, and teachers. Have students imagine that they're comparing their schedules with that of a good friend. Have each student write a note to his or her friend, summarizing when the different classes meet.

Purpose To practice writing about schedules. The targeted functions are talking about classes, sequencing events, and telling time.

Rationale Discussing schedules and courses is an everyday skill that students will want to learn so that they can talk to each other about their daily lives.

Materials Paper, pens, pencils, blank class schedules.

Portfolio Item The written class schedule and the follow-up note can both be a part of the student's written portfolio.

Oral: Repaso Activity 3, p. 92, *Pupil's Edition*

Expanded Activity The oral activity is an extension of the writing portfolio suggestion. Students exchange schedules with another student. They read their partner's schedule, and then talk with that person about what is in the schedule. They should find out why their partner is taking certain classes, which ones he or she likes or dislikes, and then see if they agree with their partner's likes and dislikes. Have them figure out if they and their partner are taking any of the same classes at the same time, if their opinions about these classes are the same, and if they have the same opinions about the teachers. Have them record their conversation.

Purpose To practice talking about class schedules and likes and dislikes. The targeted functions are talking about class schedules, sequencing events, telling time, and talking about things you like and explaining why.

Rationale Being able to communicate schedules and sequence events is essential as people juggle and coordinate all they have to do.

Material Students will need paper, pens or pencils, blank class schedules, audio or video equipment, and blank cassettes.

Portfolio Item Record the conversation on audio- or videocassette for incorporation into portfolios.

# ¿Qué haces esta tarde?

Portfolio Suggestions

Written: Repaso Activity 7, p. 117, *Pupil's Edition*

Expanded Activity Have students write several everyday activities that they especially like or don't like; for example, **Me gusta ir al parque los domingos por la tarde**, or **No me gusta ir al colegio antes de las ocho de la mañana**. Each student then tells a partner what he or she likes or doesn't like to do and the partner takes notes (in Spanish), and asks questions for clarification. The partner then uses the notes to write a brief report. (Students switch roles so that each one writes a report about the other.)

Purpose To practice using the present tense, asking for clarification, and taking notes in Spanish. The targeted function is talking about what you like or don't like to do.

Rationale Gathering information and then writing about it is a general skill that students can use in other subject areas.

Materials No special materials needed.

Portfolio Item Students may include in their writing portfolios their original written statements about themselves, their notes, or the final report about their partner.

Oral: Activity 30, p. 113, *Pupil's Edition*

Expanded Activity Have the entire class work together to create a list of ten days and times that would fall during free time. For example, one might say **los viernes a las cinco de la tarde**. Write the list on the board. Group the students into pairs. One student writes the first five times and days on five small pieces of paper. The other one writes the last five. The papers are folded and put into a hat. Pairs take turns drawing these numbers and asking a question with the day and time; for example, **¿Dónde estás los viernes a las cinco de la tarde?** The partner answers, **Estoy...**, telling where he or she usually is at that time. The partner who asks the question is the only one to see the paper. If the other partner doesn't understand, he or she needs to ask for clarification.

Purpose To practice asking and listening to questions and responding appropriately. The targeted functions are discussing what you and others do during free time and talking about where you and others go during free time.

Rationale Asking questions and responding appropriately are skills that need to be developed over a long time and should be repeated frequently.

Materials Paper and pens, small pieces of paper, and something for a hat. Audio or video recording equipment.

Portfolio Item Students may want to record the conversation and place it in the oral portfolio.

CAPÍTULO 5 — El ritmo de la vida

Portfolio Suggestions

Written: Repaso Activity 4, p. 144, *Pupil's Edition*

Expanded Activity Each student prepares a calendar, using a different page for each day of the week. Each page should be illustrated with activities that the student does on that particular day. Illustrations may include personal photos, pictures from magazines, or drawings. Each one should have a caption. The student may want to have other writing on the page. The calendars are displayed around the room in anticipation of the second step of this activity, the oral portfolio assignment.

Purpose To practice talking about different activities and relating them to times and days when one does those activities. The targeted functions are discussing how often you do things and talking about what you and your friends like to do together.

Rationale Using the newly acquired expressions to talk about the students' favorite activities will encourage them to learn the target language.

Materials Markers, glue, scissors, magazines (for pictures), paper, and pen or pencil.

Portfolio Item The calendar should be kept as part of the student's written portfolio.

Oral: Activity 30, p. 141, *Pupil's Edition*

Expanded Activity Have students prepare posters that depict their favorite season. The posters should be illustrated with different activities the student enjoys in that season. Illustrations may include photos, pictures from magazines, or drawings. Each one should have a caption. When the posters are finished, pairs of students interview each other about the posters: which season is depicted, why that season is the favorite, and how the illustrations show this. Each student asks questions, takes notes, and uses the notes to write a report about what the other student has said. Students then switch roles. Posters might be left up in the classroom for a week or so to stimulate conversation among the students.

Purpose To practice talking about seasonal activities and the weather, listening to people talk about how they spend their time, making notes of a conversation, and writing about it in the third person. The targeted functions are discussing when and how often you do things and what you and your friends like to do together.

Rationale Students need to practice listening carefully, taking notes, and clarifying information.

Materials Poster board, photos or pictures from magazines, paper, pen, pencil, audio or video recording equipment.

Portfolio Item Record students interviewing each other while referring to the posters.

Entre familia

Portfolio Suggestions

Written: Repaso Activity 7, p. 171, *Pupil's Edition*

Expanded Activity Have the entire class brainstorm to create a list of things the students want to know about their classmates' activities with friends and family. For example, ¿Cómo es un fin de semana normal en tu casa? ¿Cuántas veces a la semana comes con tu familia? ¿Cuántas veces a la semana sales con amigos? When students have created a number of questions that they can ask each other, have them use the questions to make a questionnaire. Students may then interview members of the opposite sex. There should be at least four respondents on each questionnaire.

Purpose To practice writing and talking about real-life activities. The targeted function is discussing things a family does together.

Rationale Writing and talking about their lives will motivate students to use the language.

Materials No special materials needed.

Portfolio Item A copy of the completed questionnaire can be added to the student's writing portfolio.

Oral: Activity 22, p. 161, *Pupil's Edition*

Expanded Activity Have students write about what they'd like and not like to do on their birthday or some other special day. After students write about their day, have them get into groups and compare what they like and don't like to do. Each group should then agree on how to spend a day together.

Purpose To talk about activities one does with family and friends. The targeted functions are describing a family, describing people, and discussing things a family does together.

Rationale Putting daily activities into Spanish allows students frequent use of targeted language.

Material Audio or video recording equipment. (You may want to set the classroom up to resemble a TV studio with the name of the show written on or over the set—this could be a large table with chairs arranged in a U-shape. If the class is large, this activity can be done in two or more groups.)

Portfolio Item A video recording of the mock TV show could be placed in each student's oral portfolio.

CAPÍTULO 7 ¿Qué te gustaría hacer?

Portfolio Suggestions

Written: Repaso Activity 4, p. 198, *Pupil's Edition*

Expanded Activity Students work in pairs. Student 1 talks about plans for the upcoming weekend, while Student 2 takes notes. Then Student 2 talks about his or her plans while Student 1 takes notes. Each student then writes a short paper describing his or her own plans and comparing them to his or her partner's. For example, **El viernes por la noche voy al partido de fútbol americano, pero María va a estudiar. El sábado vamos al centro comercial juntos.**

Purpose To practice vocabulary and functional expressions for making plans, listening and taking notes, rewriting notes as complete sentences.

Rationale This activity provides another opportunity to use the newly acquired target language in a real life context.

Materials No special materials needed.

Portfolio Item The paper describing weekend activities and comparing them to a partner's can be placed in the writing portfolio.

Oral: Repaso Activity 1, p. 198, *Pupil's Edition*

Expanded Activity Using the information gathered in the writing assignment, the same partners work together. Student 1 makes a "phone call" to Student 2, telling Student 2 about his or her weekend plans and inviting Student 2 to come along on one or two of the activities. If Student 2 says no, he or she must decline politely and make an excuse. If Student 2 accepts, the two will make plans to meet at a particular place and time. When the first conversation is finished, students switch roles.

Purpose To practice talking on the telephone. The targeted functions are talking on the telephone, extending and accepting invitations, making plans, turning down an invitation and making an excuse.

Rationale Talking on the phone is one of the most challenging communicative situations students will encounter. This activity gives them an opportunity to practice doing that and also to practice telephone courtesy.

Materials Two phones, two chairs, video or audio recording equipment.

Portfolio Item The final version of the telephone conversation can be recorded either on audio- or videocassette and can be added to the oral portfolio.

¡A comer!

Portfolio Suggestions

Written: Repaso Activity 7, p. 225, *Pupil's Edition*

Expanded Activity Have students work in groups of three or four to create several different types of dining situations; for example, a fast food place, an elegant restaurant, or a café. Each group should make a menu for their restaurant and, if appropriate, use poster board to create signs that advertise specials. Menus should include food by categories with prices and brief descriptions of each dish.

Purpose To practice food vocabulary. The targeted function is talking about meals and food.

Rationale One of the basic needs students will have if they visit a Spanish-speaking country is buying and ordering food. This activity will give them an opportunity to practice this vocabulary in an authentic context.

Materials Poster board, markers, colored construction paper, pens, and glue sticks.

Portfolio Item The completed menus can be placed in the writing portfolios.

Oral: Repaso Activity 3, p. 224, *Pupil's Edition*

Expanded Activity Each group should expand on what they created in the written activity by adding tables, chairs, decorations, salt and pepper shakers, etc. Then, using the menus from the written activity, have students play the roles of waitperson and customers. The customers ask for advice about different items on the menu. The waitperson responds with his or her knowledge of the menu. The waitperson then serves the food. The customers make various comments about the food, and the waitperson checks to make sure everything is all right. Finally, customers ask for the check, pay and leave, bidding the waitperson goodbye while the waitperson thanks them for their business.

Purpose To practice the targeted functions of talking about meals and food, commenting on food, making polite requests, ordering dinner in a restaurant, asking for and paying the bill in a restaurant.

Rationale Knowing restaurant etiquette and using correct language in a restaurant are essential skills.

Materials Tables, chairs, menus and items for the table such as a tablecloth, silverware, and napkins, as well as decorations. Students may also want to use glasses with water and plates with some kind of food to simulate the dishes ordered, and video or audio recorder and player.

Portfolio Item The restaurant role-play can be recorded either on audio- or videocassette. The cassette can become part of the oral portfolio.

¡Ven conmigo! Level 1 Assessment Guide **21**

CAPÍTULO 9 ¡Vamos de compras!

Portfolio Suggestions

Written: Repaso Activity 7, p. 253, *Pupil's Edition*

Expanded Activity Have students work with partners to create a page from a clothing catalog. Students can work with catalogs, magazines, or their own drawings to illustrate their clothing choices. They should write a brief description of each item, including color, style, material, size, and cost. Encourage students to use their imagination and creativity in laying out the page. When the catalog page is complete, have students create an order form for the clothing items pictured.

Purpose To practice vocabulary about clothes, colors, styles, sizes, preferences, and appearance. The targeted functions are commenting on clothes and asking about prices.

Rationale Clothing is an important topic for most teens. An activity that enables them to use clothing vocabulary and expressions will be motivating to them.

Materials Catalogs and magazines for pictures, scissors, glue, felt-tipped pens, notebook or other paper for the order form, pens, and pencils.

Portfolio Item The completed catalog page and order form can be added to the writing portfolio.

Oral: Repaso Activity 5, p. 253, *Pupil's Edition*

Expanded Activity Pairs of students exchange catalog pages. One student in the pair plays the operator at the catalog store and has a blank order form. The other student is the customer who calls to order several items. Each student should be able to see the catalog page, but students should not be able to see each other while they are talking. When the first student's order has been placed, students should switch roles and place another order.

Purpose To practice discussing clothing items, colors, styles, sizes, cost, and to practice talking on the phone. The targeted functions are commenting on clothes and asking about prices.

Rationale Reinforcing vocabulary and functional expressions about clothes will be motivating to students. Knowing how to talk on the phone is a valuable skill for students to master.

Materials Two telephones, catalog pages and order forms, audio or video recording equipment.

Portfolio Item The recorded conversation (audio or visual) can be added to the oral portfolio.

CAPÍTULO 10 Celebraciones

Portfolio Suggestions

Written: Activity 7, p. 262, *Pupil's Edition*

Expanded Activity Students work in groups in order to share supplies, but work on their own to create greeting cards for various occasions. The whole class should choose two occasions for which everyone will make a card (perhaps a holiday or a birthday), but students can also create one or two cards for special or silly occasions, such as the first day of school (or vacation), a new haircut, or the day someone finally cleaned his or her room. The entire class should discuss how they would like to display their cards before they go into the portfolios.

Purpose To practice functional expressions used with various special occasions; to become familiar with symbols used in Spanish-speaking cultures for various special occasions.

Rationale Greeting cards often use idioms and culture-specific references that are difficult for those outside the language and culture to understand. This is a good way to expose students to some of those idioms.

Materials Colored construction paper and white paper, scissors, glue, and markers.

Portfolio Item The finished cards can be placed in the writing portfolio.

Oral: Repaso Activity 8, p. 279, *Pupil's Edition*

Expanded Activity Small groups of students choose a card from the writing portfolio activity and discuss an appropriate party for that occasion. They should discuss whom they will invite, what kind of food they will serve, when and where the party will be, whether or not guests should wear special clothes, such as costumes. They should agree on a realistic budget and talk about decorations, food, etc. When the class has heard each group's party plan, they might want to actually have the party. This could be really fun if it leads to having a Christmas party in June or a party to celebrate a new haircut!

Purpose To talk about holidays and special occasions, to ask for and give opinions, to talk about food, drink, time, clothes, and money.

Rationale Students need to practice listening and responding to each other in a group, and using the newly-acquired expressions to make plans for an actual party will be motivating.

Materials Pencils and paper, audio or video recording equipment.

Portfolio Item A recording of the conversation while students are planning the party can be placed in the oral portfolio.

Para vivir bien

Portfolio Suggestions

Written: Activity 31, p. 302, *Pupil's Edition*

Expanded Activity Students work individually using the pictures on p. 302 or other pictures the teacher may want to supply. The student chooses one picture and writes a story about that person's day. Students should use tenses for the past and present and then predict what the person is going to do after each action pictured. Students should name the person(s) in the picture and give a context: Who is in the picture? What is the activity? What prior events lead up to this moment? What is the time of day, the date, the season? How and why is this sequence of events taking place? Encourage students to describe the person(s) in the photo as fully and realistically as they can.

Purpose To practice using verb tenses, to use critical thinking skills of inference and predicting, to talk about moods and physical condition. The targeted functions are saying what the person(s) in the photo did, where they went and when.

Rationale In this activity students are given the opportunity to use their critical thinking skills in target language and to integrate previously learned language skills with more recently learned ones. These two things will help them achieve proficiency.

Materials No special materials needed.

Portfolio Item The finished story along with a copy of the pictures can be placed in the writing portfolio.

Oral: Repaso Activity 3, p. 308, *Pupil's Edition*

Expanded Activity Pairs of students write various ailments on small slips of paper. There should be twelve slips of paper in all. The papers are folded and put in a hat to be drawn at random during the role-play. One student will play the doctor, the other the patient. The patient draws three ailments from the hat and pays a visit to the doctor to seek help with these problems. The students should greet each other as they would in a doctor's office. The doctor asks questions and the patient responds. The doctor should suggest a course of treatment for each problem, then the two say goodbye. The students then switch roles and a new set of ailments is drawn from the nine remaining in the hat. If the class is small and there is time, you may wish for students to use the remaining six slips of paper for a second visit to the doctor. Before recording the visit, they can then choose the three they prefer.

Purpose To practice using the present and past tense, to practice listening and responding. The targeted functions are talking about physical conditions, making suggestions, expressing feelings, and saying what you did.

Rationale In this activity students practice listening to each other and exchanging real and meaningful information based on an authentic situation.

Materials Paper and pens or pencils, classroom furniture arranged to simulate a doctor's office, video or audio recording equipment.

Portfolio Item A recording (audio or video) of the role-play can become part of the oral portfolio.

# Las vacaciones ideales

 Portfolio Suggestions

Note: In this chapter, the oral activity should precede the written activity.

Oral: Repaso Activity 3, p. 332, *Pupil's Edition*

Expanded Activity Pairs of students play a traveler and a travel agent. The traveler tells the agent in what kind of vacation he or she is interested as the agent takes notes. They then discuss possible destinations and talk about details, such as transportation, activities, and costs. When the traveler has made a final decision and they have made all of the arrangements (dates, times, tickets, hotels, activities), the travel agent should write an itinerary in a formal report and give it to the client. Students then exchange roles and repeat the process.

Purpose To practice verb tenses and vacation-related vocabulary. The targeted functions are talking about what you do and discussing what you would like to do on vacation.

Rationale Students need to be able to express their personal preferences and wishes using the target language.

Materials Posters and other visual aids to create a travel agency in the classroom, furniture arranged to simulate a travel office, audio or video recording equipment. (Posters can be obtained from a travel agency or from an airline company. They could be created by the students themselves, perhaps in collaboration with the art teacher.)

Portfolio Item An audio or video recording of the conversation between the client and the travel agent can be placed in each student's oral portfolio.

Written: Activity 18, p. 323, *Pupil's Edition*

Expanded Activity With the itinerary written out by the travel agent, each traveler creates three picture postcards to send back from the vacation that was planned in the oral activity. Students can draw pictures or use pictures from magazines or travel brochures to create the postcard. The other side of the card should be written from the destination using present progressive to report on what the student is doing at that moment.

Purpose To practice appropriate vacation-related expressions and vocabulary. The targeted function is talking about what you are doing on vacation.

Rationale Practice appropriate uses of verb tenses.

Materials 4 x 6 index cards, magazines or brochures, scissors, glue, felt-tipped pens, pen or pencil.

Portfolio Item The three postcards can be added to the student's writing portfolio.

To the Teacher

Speaking Tests

The primary goal of **¡Ven conmigo!** is to help students develop proficiency in Spanish. The speaking tests in the *Assessment Guide* have been designed to help assess students' proficiency in listening to and speaking Spanish. The speaking tests, which measure how well students use the language in contexts that approximate real-life situations, reflect the interview/role-play format of the Situation Cards in the *Chapter Resource Books*. You can choose whether to set up interviews with each student, role-play the short situations with individual students, or have pairs of students role-play the situations spontaneously as you observe.

Administering a speaking test requires approximately three to five minutes with each student or pair of students. You might administer a speaking test to one student or pair while the others are working on the reading and writing sections of a Chapter Test. Make sure that you and the student(s) are seated far enough from the others so that they will not be disturbed. Instruct the student(s) to speak in a soft but audible voice. If such an arrangement is not possible, meet with students at mutually agreed upon times outside class.

The Speaking Test Evaluation Form on page 27 will help you assess each student's performance. At the end of each test, take a moment to note your impression of the student's performance on the evaluation form. The following guidelines offer one possibility for assessing a student's global score, based on this evaluation.

18–20 pts: The student accomplishes the assigned task successfully, speaks clearly and accurately, and brings additional linguistic material to the basic situation, for example, using new functions or structures that beginning language learners seldom use spontaneously.

16–17 pts: The student accomplishes the assigned task successfully with a few errors. The student is able to communicate effectively in spite of these errors and offers meaningful responses.

14–15 pts: The student accomplishes the task with difficulty. He or she demonstrates minimum oral competence, hesitates frequently, and shows little creativity, offering only minimal, predictable responses.

12–13 pts: The student is unable to accomplish the task or fails to demonstrate acceptable mastery of functions, vocabulary, and grammatical concepts.

0–11 pts: Communication is almost non-existent. The student does not understand the aural cues and is unable to accomplish the task. Errors are so extreme that communication is impossible.

Nombre _____ Clase _____ Fecha _____

Speaking Test Evaluation Form

Chapter _____ ☐ Interview   ☐ Role-play   ☐ Other format

Targeted Function(s) _____
_____
_____

Context (Topic) _____

COMPREHENSION (ability to understand aural cues and respond appropriately)	(POOR) 1 2 3 4 (EXCELLENT)	
COMPREHENSIBILITY (ability to communicate ideas and be understood)	(POOR) 1 2 3 4 (EXCELLENT)	
ACCURACY (ability to use structures and vocabulary correctly)	(POOR) 1 2 3 4 (EXCELLENT)	
FLUENCY (ability to communicate clearly and smoothly)	(POOR) 1 2 3 4 (EXCELLENT)	
EFFORT (inclusion of details beyond the minimum predictable response)	(POOR) 1 2 3 4 (EXCELLENT)	

TOTAL POINTS ☐

NOTES:
_____
_____
_____
_____
_____

¡Ven conmigo! Level 1

¡Mucho gusto!

Speaking Test

Targeted Functions: saying hello and goodbye; introducing people and responding to an introduction; asking how someone is and saying how you are; asking and saying how old someone is; asking where someone is from and saying where you're from; talking about likes and dislikes

A. Interview
Have students respond to the following in Spanish.
1. ¿Cómo te llamas?
2. ¿De dónde eres?
3. Hola. ¿Cómo estás?
4. ¿Cuántos años tienes?
5. ¿Qué te gusta más, la música clásica o la música rock?

B. Role-play
Have pairs of students act out the following situation. You can also act it out with individual students.

> You're a reporter for the school newspaper who is interviewing an exchange student from Spain. Greet the student, introduce yourself, and find out his or her name, age, and at least two likes and dislikes. End your conversation with an appropriate goodbye.

¡Organízate!

Speaking Test

Targeted Functions: talking about what you want and need; describing the contents of your room; talking about what you need and want to do

A. Interview
Have students respond to the following in Spanish.
1. ¿Qué necesitas para tus clases?
2. ¿Qué hay en tu cuarto?
3. ¿Qué hay en la clase de español?
4. ¿Necesitas ir al centro comercial?
5. ¿Qué quieres comprar para tus clases?

B. Role-play
Have pairs of students act out the following situation. You can also act it out with individual students.

> You need to go shopping for school supplies. First make a list of all the items you need, then go shopping. Tell the salesperson the items and quantities you need and he or she will tell you if the items are in stock and how much each item costs.

CAPÍTULO 3: Nuevas clases, nuevos amigos

Speaking Test

Targeted Functions: talking about classes and sequencing events; telling time; telling at what time something happens; talking about being late or in a hurry; describing people and things; talking about things you like and explaining why

A. Interview
Have students respond to the following in Spanish.
1. ¿Qué hora es?
2. ¿A qué hora es la clase de español?
3. ¿Qué clases tienes hoy?
4. ¿Cómo son tus compañeros?
5. ¿Cuál es tu clase favorita? ¿Por qué?

B. Role-play
Have pairs of students act out the following situation. You can also act it out with individual students.

You have just received your new schedule for the semester. You meet your friend and discuss which classes you have and what times they meet. Tell why you like or don't like your schedule.

CAPÍTULO 4: ¿Qué haces esta tarde?

Speaking Test

Targeted Functions: talking about what you like to do; discussing what you and others do during free time; telling where people and things are; talking about where you and others go during free time

A. Interview
Have students respond to the following in Spanish.
1. ¿Qué te gusta hacer cuando estás en casa?
2. ¿Qué haces los sábados con tus amigos?
3. ¿Practicas los deportes? Cuáles?
4. ¿Dónde está el parque?
5. ¿Adónde vas con tu familia los fines de semana?

B. Role-play
Have pairs of students act out the following situation. You can also act it out with individual students.

You and a friend meet after school to talk about what to do this weekend. One of you will ask, **¿Qué haces este fin de semana?** You respond and ask your friend the same question. Talk about what things you like and don't like to do. Each of you should ask and answer at least five questions.

CAPÍTULO 5 — El ritmo de la vida

Speaking Test

Targeted Functions: discussing how often you do things; talking about what you and your friends like to do together; talking about what you do during a typical week; giving today's date; talking about the weather

A. Interview
Have your students respond to the following in Spanish.
1. ¿Qué tiempo hace hoy?
2. ¿Qué te gusta hacer cuando hace frío?
3. ¿Cuál es la fecha?
4. ¿Con qué frecuencia lees el periódico?
5. ¿Les gusta a Uds. asistir a conciertos de _____?
   (Choose current musical group)

B. Role-play
Have pairs of students act out the following situation. You can also act it out with individual students.

> You and a friend are trying to figure out what to do together. Your friend will ask, **¿Qué te gusta hacer cuando hace _____?** (He or she will give a weather expression.). You respond and ask your friend the same question. Discuss what activities you like and don't like to do in various weather conditions or seasons. Each of you should ask and answer at least five questions.

CAPÍTULO 6 — Entre familia

Speaking Test

Targeted Functions: describing a family; describing people; discussing things a family does together; discussing problems and giving advice

A. Interview
Have students respond to the following in Spanish.
1. ¿Cuántas personas hay en tu familia?
2. ¿Cómo son tus hermanos?
3. ¿De qué color es tu pelo? ¿tus ojos?
4. ¿Qué hacen Uds., tú y tu familia, juntos?
5. ¿Qué debes hacer para ayudar en casa?

B. Role-play
Have pairs of students act out the following situation. You can also act it out with individual students.

> You and a friend are talking about how overworked your parents are. You decide that it would be a good idea to do something to help out. One of you starts the conversation with **Pobrecitos de mis padres. Ellos trabajan demasiado.** The other person inquires what your parents do and then gives advice about how to help. Each of you suggests three things that other members of the family should do to help.

CAPÍTULO 7 ¿Qué te gustaría hacer?

Speaking Test

Targeted Functions: talking on the telephone; extending and accepting invitations; making plans; talking about getting ready; turning down an invitation and making an excuse

A. Interview
Have students respond to the following in Spanish.
1. ¿Te gustaría ir al circo conmigo?
2. ¿Qué piensas hacer el viernes?
3. ¿Tienes ganas de estudiar o ir al acuario?
4. ¿Cuándo necesitas maquillarte/afeitarte?
5. ¿Ya tienes planes o quieres ir a una fiesta mañana?

B. Role-play
Have pairs of students act out the following situation. You can also act it out with individual students.

> Imagine that you're calling a friend to invite him or her to a surprise party you are throwing. Your friend will either accept the invitation and ask more about the party, or decline the invitation and give an appropriate, polite excuse and tell you what he or she is planning to do instead.

CAPÍTULO 8 ¡A comer!

Speaking Test

Targeted Functions: talking about meals and food; commenting on food; making polite requests; ordering dinner in a restaurant; asking for and paying the bill in a restaurant

A. Interview
Have students respond to the following in Spanish.
1. ¿Qué te gusta comer para el desayuno? ¿Y para el almuerzo?
2. ¿Cómo está la comida de la cafetería?
3. ¿Cuál es más salado, las papitas o el pan dulce?
4. Cuando vas a un restaurante, ¿qué pides? ¿Quién paga la cuenta?
5. ¿Cuál es tu plato favorito? ¿Por qué?

B. Role-play
Have pairs of students act out the following situation. You can also act it out with individual students.

> You are at a restaurant. Order what you want to eat and drink, comment on the food, and pay the bill. Remember to be polite when speaking with the waiter or waitress, and don't forget to ask if the tip is included.

¡Vamos de compras!

Speaking Test

Targeted Functions: discussing gift suggestions; asking for and giving directions downtown; commenting on clothes; making comparisons; expressing preferences; asking about prices and paying for something

A. Interview
Have students respond to the following in Spanish.
1. ¿Qué piensas regalarle a tu mamá para su cumpleaños?
2. ¿Me puede decir dónde está el centro comercial en esta ciudad?
3. ¿Prefieres llevar botas o zapatos de tenis? ¿Por qué?
4. ¿Qué ropa llevas cuando vas a una fiesta?
5. ¿Son más caras las camisetas o las blusas de seda? ¿Cuánto cuestan?

B. Role-play
Have pairs of students act out the following situation. You can also act it out with individual students.

> You are in a store shopping for clothes to wear to a party this weekend. Tell the salesperson what you're looking for and find out if they have it in a certain material and color. Ask how much it costs and then tell the salesperson if you're going to buy it or not. If you decide to buy it, pay for it at the cashier.

Celebraciones

Speaking Test

Targeted Functions: talking about what you're doing right now; asking for and giving an opinion; asking for help and responding to requests; telling a friend what to do; talking about past events

A. Interview
Have students respond to the following in Spanish.
1. ¿Qué estás haciendo?
2. ¿Qué te parece si vamos al cine esta noche?
3. ¿Me puedes ayudar a decorar la clase?
4. ¿Cuál es tu día festivo favorito? ¿Por qué?
5. ¿Quién preparó la cena anoche?

B. Role-play
Have pairs of students act out the following situation. You can also act it out with individual students.

> You and a friend are planning a graduation party for another friend. Exchange ideas about what kind of gift to buy and decide who will do what to prepare for the party.

Para vivir bien

Speaking Test

Targeted Functions: making suggestions and expressing feelings, talking about moods and physical condition; saying what you did; talking about where you went and when

A. Interview
Have students respond to the following in Spanish.
1. ¿Cómo estás? ¿Cómo te sientes hoy?
2. ¿Qué le pasa a tu mejor amigo(a)? ¿Está enfermo(a)?
3. ¿Por qué no vas al partido el viernes?
4. ¿Qué hiciste ayer?
5. ¿Adónde fueron tú y tu familia el fin de semana pasado?

B. Role-play
Have pairs of students act out the following situation. You can also act it out with individual students.

> You are being interviewed for membership in a health club. The interviewer will ask you questions about your medical history and what you normally do to stay healthy. Answer the questions and make comments about how important you think the following things are: eating right, exercising regularly, etc. Mention in your discussion how your health and fitness affects your overall well-being.

Las vacaciones ideales

Speaking Test

Targeted Functions: talking about what you do and like to do every day; making future plans; discussing what you would like to do on vacation; saying where you went and what you did on vacation

A. Interview
Have students respond to the following in Spanish.
1. Por lo general, ¿qué haces durante la semana?
2. ¿Qué piensas hacer durante el verano?
3. ¿Te gustaría viajar a México? ¿Por qué sí o por qué no?
4. ¿Adónde fueron tú y tu familia durante las vacaciones?
5. ¿Qué hicieron? ¿Nadaron? ¿Montaron en bicicleta?

B. Role-play
Have pairs of students act out the following situation. You can also act it out with individual students.

> You have just won a dream vacation and your friend wants to know all about it! He or she wants to know where you are going, what you plan to do there, and why you chose that particular place. After you have answered your friend's questions, find out if he or she would like to do the same things.

ASSESSMENT

Midterm and Final Examinations

Midterm Exam 35–42

Score Sheet for Midterm Exam 43–45

Listening Scripts for Midterm Exam 46–47

Answers to Midterm Exam 48

Final Exam 49–56

Score Sheet for Final Exam 57–59

Listening Scripts for Final Exam 60–61

Answers to Final Exam 62

Nombre _____ Clase _____ Fecha _____

Midterm Exam Capítulos 1–6

I. Listening
Maximum Score: 20 points

A. Listen as Gloria and Juan discuss their school subjects. Then answer the following questions based on their conversation. (5 points)

_____ 1. ¿Cómo está Gloria?
   a. bastante mal
   b. rubia
   c. bien

_____ 2. ¿Qué clase le gusta a Juan?
   a. inglés
   b. francés
   c. biología

_____ 3. ¿Por qué no le gusta a Gloria la clase de francés?
   a. Es mala.
   b. Es aburrida.
   c. Es interesante.

_____ 4. ¿A qué hora es la clase de francés?
   a. A la una.
   b. Son las ocho.
   c. A las ocho.

_____ 5. Juan tiene prisa porque su clase de baile está _____.
   a. bastante lejos
   b. atrasada
   c. muy cerca

SCORE [ ]

B. Listen to the following statements and decide if they are **a) logical** or **b) illogical**. (5 points)

_____ 6.

_____ 7.

_____ 8.

_____ 9.

_____ 10.

SCORE [ ]

¡Ven conmigo! Level 1   Assessment Guide **35**

Nombre _____ Clase _____ Fecha _____

C. What is everybody talking about? Match each topic with the correct conversation.
(5 points)

_____ 11.
_____ 12.
_____ 13.
_____ 14.
_____ 15.

a. free-time activities
b. family members
c. household chores
d. school subjects
e. the weather

SCORE [ ]

D. Listen as Mercedes describes her friends. Then match each name with the correct picture.
(5 points)

a.   b.   c.   d.   e.

_____ 16. Luisa
_____ 17. Mario
_____ 18. Beto
_____ 19. Dolores
_____ 20. Jaime

SCORE [ ]

II. Reading

Maximum Score: 25 points

A. Read the following questions and choose the best answer for each one. (5 points)

_____ 21. ¿Cuántos años tienes?
_____ 22. ¿Qué les gusta hacer después de clases?
_____ 23. ¿De dónde es Maribel?
_____ 24. ¿Qué tiempo hace?
_____ 25. ¿Cómo te llamas?

a. Es de Sevilla.
b. Margarita, ¿y tú?
c. Está lloviendo.
d. Tengo quince años.
e. Nos gusta ir al centro comercial.

SCORE [ ]

36 Assessment Guide   ¡Ven conmigo! Level 1

Nombre _____ Clase _____ Fecha _____

B. Juan and Ana meet in the hallway after school. Put their conversation in the correct order. (5 points)

_____ 26.
_____ 27.
_____ 28.
_____ 29.
_____ 30.

a. ¿Historia? Yo también. ¿Por qué no estudiamos juntos? Es más divertido, ¿no?
b. Hola, Juan. ¿Qué tal?
c. ¡Buena idea! ¡Vamos!
d. Yo necesito estudiar también porque tengo un examen de historia mañana.
e. Regular. Tengo dos exámenes mañana. Necesito estudiar pero no quiero.

SCORE _____

C. Read about Amalia's family. Then decide if the statements that follow are **a) true** or **b) false**. (5 points)

Amalia tiene una familia bastante grande y unida. Tiene una hermana menor, abuelos y muchos tíos y primos. Todos viven en la misma ciudad. Sus abuelos viven al lado de la familia. Tío Jaime y tía Adriana viven muy cerca también en una casa grande con una piscina. Tienen tres hijos — Marcos, Patricia y Cristina. Tía Luisa no tiene hijos, pero tiene dos perros y un gato. Es profesora de inglés. Toda la familia visita a los abuelos los domingos por la tarde. Además, cada invierno todos, la familia de Amalia, los abuelos, los tíos y los primos hacen un viaje a las montañas de Colorado. A todos les gusta esquiar aunque el papá de Amalia no sabe esquiar muy bien. Amalia tiene una hermana menor que se llama Josefina. A Josefina le gusta asistir a la escuela y practicar los deportes.

_____ 31. Amalia's family likes to do things together.

_____ 32. One of Amalia's uncles teaches English.

_____ 33. Amalia rarely sees her grandparents.

_____ 34. Josefina is younger than Amalia.

_____ 35. No one in Amalia's family likes cold weather.

SCORE _____

¡Ven conmigo! Level 1

Nombre _____ Clase _____ Fecha _____

D. Look at this TV guide and decide if the statements below are **a) true** or **b) false**. The times are based on a twenty-four-hour clock, so that 13:00 is 1:00 p.m., for example. (5 points)

6:00 6:30	Buenos días agricultor	Despertares Esta mañana	Noticiero Telem.	NBC News	Dibujos Club 700	Buenos días Euronews
7:00 7:30	Primera hora Protagonistas	Deporte total	La noticia Copa	Contacto directo	Noti 10	Aprendiendo a vivir Noticiero
8:00 8:30	Mucho gusto	Vanidades Teve	Club telemundo	Tiro libre Complicidades	Acción de Noti 10 D'Cocina	Telediario Telenegocios
9:00 9:30	Para usted Dibujos	Toque de Mariaca Cine: A veces se	Animados	Gino Mollinari	El mundo infantil de TC	Directo Tve TV mandato
10:00 10:30	Clásicos del cine mexicano	dice una mentira		Princesa		Euronews TV mandato
11:00 11:30		La traidora	Cara a cara: Me visto como me	Por estas calles	TC cine: Idilio presente	Mundo de cada día Primera respuesta
12:00 12:30	Gasparín Protagonistas	Deporte total	da la gana Primer impacto	Telebreves Bonanza		Lingo
13:00 13:30	Polivoces Medio día	24 horas	El Pirrurris Aló que tal	Televistazo Video Show	Noti 10 Sintonizando	Telenegocios Deutsche Welle
14:00 14:30	En familia con Mercedes	Aquí Mariela Marielena		Cuando llega el	Geraldo: Los	Tventas Aventura del saber
15:00 15:30	Alcanzar una estrella	Inés Duarte	Ocurrió así	amor Señora	dobles de los famosos	
16:00 16:30	Deportes espectaculares	Club de Disney	Cristina	Liveman	El engaño	Sinvergüenza Deutsche welle
17:00 17:30	Supercampeones	Carrusel	Feria de la alegría	Yo amo a Lucy Chapulín	Potra Zaina	TV mandato

"Teleagenda" from *Hoy*, Tuesday, May 3, 1994. Copyright © 1994 by Editores e Impresores S.A. Reprinted by permission of **Editores e Impresores S.A.**

_____ 36. Si te interesan el tenis, el fútbol, etc., hay un programa interesante a las siete y media de la mañana.

_____ 37. Si quieres ver una película, debes mirar la tele a las diez de la mañana.

_____ 38. *Geraldo* es a las cuatro de la tarde.

_____ 39. El programa antes de *Para usted* se llama *Mucho gusto*.

_____ 40. Te gustan los videos; a la una y media hay un programa para ti.

SCORE _____

E. Read the descriptions of Guillermo's classmates on page 39. Then match each drawing with the passage that correctly describes each person. (5 points)

a.   b.   c.   d.   e.

Nombre _____ Clase _____ Fecha _____

_____ 41. Mi amigo David es muy alto y delgado. Le gustan muchos deportes, por ejemplo, el fútbol, el tenis y la natación. Todos los fines de semana va al parque a jugar al tenis.

_____ 42. A Pat le encanta la música clásica. Es inteligente y muy trabajadora. Toca la guitarra muy bien porque practica todos los días.

_____ 43. Eugenio es moreno y muy atlético. Practica deportes después de clases con sus amigos. Ahora está en el parque.

_____ 44. Chris es buen cocinero y ayuda a preparar la comida en casa. Me gusta comer todo lo que prepara.

_____ 45. Marcos es guapo y romántico. Tiene muchos amigos y a ellos les gusta cantar mientras Marcos toca sus canciones favoritas.

SCORE _____

III. Culture

Maximum Score: 10 points

A. Read the statements below. Based on the information in your textbook, determine whether the statements are **a) true** or **b) false**. (5 points)

_____ 46. It's possible to go snow-skiing in parts of South America in July.

_____ 47. It's very common for teens in Spanish-speaking countries to get cars on their sixteenth birthdays.

_____ 48. If you looked for Francisco Javier López Aguilar in a phone book, you would look under **L**.

_____ 49. Students in Spanish-speaking countries take 5–6 classes daily, like students in the United States.

_____ 50. Most teenagers in Spanish-speaking countries have phones and TV sets in their bedrooms.

SCORE _____

B. Write five cultural facts you have learned about Spanish-speaking countries or people. You may choose from the following categories: sports, transportation, grading scales, greetings among friends, or interpersonal space. (5 points)

51. _____

52. _____

53. _____

54. _____

55. _____

SCORE _____

Nombre _____ Clase _____ Fecha _____

IV. Writing

Maximum Score: 45 points

A. For each item below, write a complete sentence in Spanish telling how you would ask for or give the information indicated. (10 points)

How would you...

56. ask a friend what the new math teacher is like
_____

57. ask a classmate if he or she likes sports
_____

58. tell your mom or dad you don't want to eat because you're not hungry
_____

59. ask what time it is
_____

60. ask a new friend how many people there are in his or her family
_____

SCORE [ ]

B. Answer the following questions in complete sentences. (10 points)

61. ¿Cuántos años tienes?
_____

62. ¿Qué te gusta hacer los fines de semana?
_____

63. ¿Qué tiempo hace hoy?
_____

64. ¿De qué color son tus ojos?
_____

65. ¿De dónde eres?
_____

SCORE [ ]

Nombre _____ Clase _____ Fecha _____

C. Look at the drawing and then answer the questions below in complete Spanish sentences. (10 points)

66. Name at least three things that are in the bedroom.
   _____

67. What is the girl in the living room doing?
   _____

68. The woman in the kitchen is preparing a meal, but what two chores should she do next?
   _____

69. What two things does the girl who is studying need to do? Her room's a mess!
   _____

70. What's the weather like today?
   _____

SCORE _____

¡Ven conmigo! Level 1 — Assessment Guide **41**

Nombre _____ Clase _____ Fecha _____

D. Write a paragraph of at least five sentences about your school. Include the following elements: where your school is in relation to your house, what time your first class starts, what your favorite class is, what your best friends are like, and what you and your friends like to do after school. (15 points)

71. _____
_____
_____
_____
_____
_____
_____
_____
_____
_____

SCORE ☐

TOTAL SCORE ☐ /100

Nombre _____ Clase _____ Fecha _____

Midterm Exam Score Sheet

Circle the letter that matches the most appropriate response.

I. Listening
Maximum Score: 20 points

A. (5 points)
1. a b c
2. a b c
3. a b c
4. a b c
5. a b c

SCORE ☐

B. (5 points)
6. a b
7. a b
8. a b
9. a b
10. a b

SCORE ☐

C. (5 points)
11. a b c d e
12. a b c d e
13. a b c d e
14. a b c d e
15. a b c d e

SCORE ☐

D. (5 points)
16. a b c d e
17. a b c d e
18. a b c d e
19. a b c d e
20. a b c d e

SCORE ☐

II. Reading
Maximum Score: 25 points

A. (5 points)
21. a b c d e
22. a b c d e
23. a b c d e
24. a b c d e
25. a b c d e

SCORE ☐

B. (5 points)
26. a b c d e
27. a b c d e
28. a b c d e
29. a b c d e
30. a b c d e

SCORE ☐

C. (5 points)
31. a b
32. a b
33. a b
34. a b
35. a b

SCORE ☐

D. (5 points)
36. a b
37. a b
38. a b
39. a b
40. a b

SCORE ☐

E. (5 points)
41. a b c d e
42. a b c d e
43. a b c d e
44. a b c d e
45. a b c d e

SCORE ☐

¡Ven conmigo! Level 1   Assessment Guide 43

Nombre _____ Clase _____ Fecha _____

III. Culture
Maximum Score: 10 points

A. (5 points)

46. a b
47. a b
48. a b
49. a b
50. a b

SCORE [ ]

B. (5 points)

51. _____
52. _____
53. _____
54. _____
55. _____

SCORE [ ]

IV. Writing
Maximum Score: 45 points

A. (10 points)

56. _____
57. _____
58. _____
59. _____
60. _____

SCORE [ ]

Nombre _____ Clase _____ Fecha _____

B. (10 points)

61. _____
62. _____
63. _____
64. _____
65. _____

SCORE ☐

C. (10 points)

66. _____
67. _____
68. _____
69. _____
70. _____

SCORE ☐

D. (15 points)

71. _____
_____
_____
_____
_____
_____
_____
_____
_____
_____
_____
_____

SCORE ☐

TOTAL SCORE ☐ /100

¡Ven conmigo! Level 1

Listening Scripts for Midterm Exam

I. Listening

A.
GLORIA ¡Hola, Juan! ¿Qué tal?
JUAN Bien, ¿y tú, Gloria?
GLORIA Estoy bien. ¿Te gustan las clases nuevas?
JUAN Sí. Mi clase favorita es la clase de inglés porque me gustan los idiomas. Y a ti, ¿te gustan tus clases?
GLORIA Sí, más o menos, pero no me gusta la clase de francés porque es muy aburrida. Además, es demasiado temprano. Es a las ocho de la mañana.
JUAN Oye, Gloria. No tengo reloj. ¿Qué hora es?
GLORIA A ver... ya son las cuatro.
JUAN Ay, estoy atrasado. Mi clase de baile es a las cuatro y media. Está muy lejos de aquí y necesito tomar el autobús.
GLORIA ¡Date prisa! Nos vemos mañana.

B.
6. Debes estudiar esta noche porque tienes un examen mañana.
7. Cuando necesito comprar cuadernos y libros voy a la librería.
8. Es divertido nadar cuando hace mucho calor.
9. Mi hermana tiene cinco años. Yo tengo quince años. Ella es mi hermana mayor.
10. Me gusta practicar deportes cuando estoy en la biblioteca.

C.
11.
ANA Juanita, ¿qué clases tienes este semestre?
JUANITA Tengo química, geometría, educación física, inglés, español y computación. ¿Y tú?
ANA Tengo álgebra, geografía, inglés, arte, ciencias sociales y francés.

12.
FELIPE Jorge, ¿ayudas mucho en casa?
JORGE Claro, hombre. Pongo la mesa, saco la basura y corto el césped.
FELIPE ¡Qué trabajador! Oye, ¿quieres limpiar mi cuarto?

13.
DINORA ¿Qué hacen ustedes después de clases?
SILVIA Depende, pero muchas veces vamos a tomar algo en un café o montamos en bicicleta.

14.
MELVIN Es un buen día para ir al parque a jugar al fútbol, ¿verdad?
ENRIQUE No, Melvin. Hace frío y va a llover.

15.
SANDRA ¿Cuántos hermanos tienes?
ERNESTO Un hermano. No tengo una familia grande. Somos cuatro—mi mamá, mi papá y mi hermano mayor.

D. MERCEDES ¿Cómo son mis amigos? A ver... Mi amiga Luisa es bonita, morena y muy activa. Le encanta bailar. Mario es alto y delgado. Le encanta jugar al baloncesto. Beto es guapo y moreno. Es un amigo muy divertido. Dolores tiene el pelo largo y es delgada. Le gusta descansar y hablar con amigos. Y Jaime, pues Jaime es mi mejor amigo. Es guapo y moreno. Todos los fines de semana montamos en bicicleta juntos.

Answers to Midterm Exam

I. Listening Maximum Score: 20 points

A. (5 points: 1 point per item)
1. c
2. a
3. b
4. c
5. a

B. (5 points: 1 point per item)
6. a
7. a
8. a
9. b
10. b

C. (5 points: 1 point per item)
11. d
12. c
13. a
14. e
15. b

D. (5 points: 1 point per item)
16. d
17. b
18. a
19. e
20. c

II. Reading Maximum Score: 25 points

A. (5 points: 1 point per item)
21. d
22. e
23. a
24. c
25. b

B. (5 points: 1 point per item)
26. b
27. e
28. d
29. a
30. c

C. (5 points: 1 point per item)
31. a
32. b
33. b
34. a
35. b

D. (5 points: 1 point per item)
36. a
37. a
38. b
39. a
40. a

E. (5 points: 1 point per item)
41. c
42. b
43. a
44. e
45. d

III. Culture Maximum Score: 10 points

A. (5 points: 1 point per item)
46. a
47. b
48. a
49. b
50. b

B. (5 points: 1 point per item)
Answers will vary for numbers 51. to 55.
Possible answers:
Soccer and tennis are popular sports in Spanish-speaking countries.
Fewer young people own cars in Spain or Latin America than in the United States.
Mexican schools use a grading scale of 1 to 10; 6 is passing.
Spanish speakers often greet each other with a handshake or a kiss.
In Spain, most people live in apartments; bedrooms are smaller and sisters or brothers will sometimes have to share a room.

IV. Writing Maximum Score: 45 points

A. (10 points: 2 points per item)
56. ¿Cómo es el/la nuevo(a) profesor(a) de matemáticas?
57. ¿Te gustan los deportes?
58. Mamá, no quiero comer porque no tengo hambre.
59. ¿Qué hora es, por favor?
60. ¿Cuántas personas hay en tu familia?

B. (10 points: 2 points per item) Answers will vary for numbers 61. to 65.

C. (10 points: 2 points per item) Answers will vary for numbers 66. to 70.

D. (15 points: 3 points per sentence) Answers will vary for number 71. Possible answers:
La escuela está cerca de mi casa. Mi primera clase comienza a las ocho y veinte. Mi clase favorita es la biología. Mis amigos son simpáticos y divertidos. Después de clases nos gusta ir a un café a tomar algo.

Nombre _____ Clase _____ Fecha _____

Final Exam Capítulos 7–12

I. Listening
Maximum Score: 30 points

A. Listen as Jorge and Marta talk about their vacation plans. Then based on their conversation, choose the best answer to each question. (5 points)

_____ 1. ¿Qué piensa hacer Marta?
  a. viajar a Puerto Rico
  b. viajar a América del Sur

_____ 2. ¿Adónde va a ir Jorge?
  a. a ningún lugar
  b. a Rio de Janeiro

_____ 3. ¿Qué piensa comprar Marta?
  a. una chaqueta y botas de cuero
  b. unos esquís y una tienda de camping

_____ 4. ¿Qué les gustaría hacer a los padres de Marta?
  a. tomar el sol
  b. hacer turismo

_____ 5. ¿Qué le gustaría hacer a la hermana de Marta?
  a. bajar el río en canoa
  b. escalar montañas

SCORE _____

B. Listen to the following statements and decide if they are **a) logical** or **b) illogical**. (10 points)

_____ 6.   _____ 11.
_____ 7.   _____ 12.
_____ 8.   _____ 13.
_____ 9.   _____ 14.
_____ 10. _____ 15.

SCORE _____

C. Listen to the following morning announcements at the Centro Unión high school. Decide if the following events, **a) have already taken place** or **b) are going to happen**. (10 points)

_____ 16.   _____ 21.
_____ 17.   _____ 22.
_____ 18.   _____ 23.
_____ 19.   _____ 24.
_____ 20.   _____ 25.

SCORE _____

¡Ven conmigo! Level 1   Assessment Guide **49**

Nombre _____ Clase _____ Fecha _____

D. Today is a very busy day in the downtown commercial area of the city. Listen to the following conversations and decide in which of the stores they are taking place. (5 points)

_____ 26.
_____ 27.
_____ 28.
_____ 29.
_____ 30.

a. Pastelería La Concha
b. Joyería La Perla
c. Florería Rosa Rojas
d. Dulcería El Cacahuate
e. Zapatería El Taconcito

SCORE ____

II. Reading

Maximum Score: 30 points

A. Read the following questions and select the best answer to each one. (5 points)

_____ 31. ¿Qué te parece si invitamos a Juan a la fiesta?

_____ 32. ¿Crees que hay bastante comida?

_____ 33. ¿Crees que mandamos bastantes invitaciones?

_____ 34. ¿Qué te parece si le pedimos a Jorge sus discos compactos?

_____ 35. ¿Daniel va a traer los refrescos?

a. Perfecto. Él tiene muy buena música.
b. Creo que sí porque él fue al supermercado por la mañana.
c. Creo que sí porque Renato y Patricia prepararon mucho arroz con pollo.
d. ¡Buena idea! Él toca muy bien la guitarra.
e. ¡Claro que sí! Todos los amigos de la escuela recibieron una.

SCORE ____

B. Find the best answer to each of the following questions. (5 points)

_____ 36. ¿Me haces el favor de llamar a Manuel?

_____ 37. ¿Me ayudas a limpiar mi cuarto?

_____ 38. ¿Me traes una silla?

_____ 39. ¿Me pasas los regalos?

_____ 40. ¿Me ayudas a decorar la sala?

a. ¡Con mucho gusto! Y luego tú me ayudas a limpiar el mío.
b. Sí, hombre. ¿Tienes los globos?
c. Claro que sí. ¿Cuál es su número de teléfono?
d. Perdóname pero no puedo. El doctor me prohibió levantar cosas pesadas *(heavy)*.
e. ¡Cómo no! ¿Qué le vas a regalar a Ana?

SCORE ____

C. Read these tips about controlling stress. Then look at the following statements about several students and decide if each one is following the article's advice. Using only the information in the article, choose a) if the student seems to be doing a good job of managing stress or b) if the student's habits could be improved. (5 points)

7 Claves para manejar el ESTRÉS

1. Comer por lo menos una comida balanceada al día. La nutrición es esencial para una buena salud y proporciona defensas contra el estrés.

2. Dormir por lo menos 8 horas cada noche. Un sueño apropiado puede añadir años de vida. Trate de acostarse y levantarse a la misma hora.

3. Hacer ejercicio, por lo menos 3 veces por semana. Busque una actividad divertida, como la bicicleta, o como caminar o nadar.

4. No debe tomar demasiada cafeína. Puede producir irritabilidad, dolor de cabeza, ansiedad y depresión.

5. Salir y cultivar sus amistades; un buen amigo es un gran soporte. Tener amigos cercanos es algo valioso; un buen amigo puede subir la moral con sólo estar presente.

6. Organizar su tiempo. Planée su uso y empléelo.

7. Sea optimista: las personas optimistas tienen menos problemas mentales y síquicos.

Adaptation from "17 Claves para manejar el Estrés" (Retitled: "7 Claves para manejar el Estrés") from *Bienestar*, no. 9. Copyright © by *Colsanitas*. Reprinted by permission of the publisher.

_____ 41. Ana Luisa se acuesta muy temprano a veces y muy tarde los fines de semana.

_____ 42. Javier tiene muchos amigos, pero Fabio es un amigo muy especial que lo ayuda mucho con sus problemas.

_____ 43. ¡Qué chico tan sistemático es Pepe! Siempre sabe exactamente lo que va a hacer y cuándo lo va a hacer.

_____ 44. Rosana es buena amiga pero me parece que siempre piensa en las cosas negativas.

_____ 45. Nora nunca desayuna pero come un almuerzo sano todos los días.

SCORE _____

Nombre _____ Clase _____ Fecha _____

D. Carlos has had a terrible day. Read the following entry in his diary and decide if the statements below are **a) true** or **b) false**. (5 points)

jueves 2 de abril

Querido diario:

Hoy fue un día horrible. Le hice cinco invitaciones a Elisa y ella me contestó que no a todas. Primero, la invité a ir al partido de fútbol conmigo mañana, y ella respondió: "¡Qué lástima! Ya tengo planes. Tal vez otro día". Luego, la invité al cine el sábado y me contestó: "Lo siento, pero tengo una cita con Pablo". Después la invité a comer pizza esta tarde y me dijo: "Me gustaría, pero no puedo. Estoy cansada y tengo sueño". Luego, la invité a ir al museo el domingo, y ella me dijo: "Lo siento, pero tengo que estudiar álgebra". Finalmente, ella me invitó a jugar al voleibol la próxima semana, ¡pero no puedo! Voy a estar en San Antonio para jugar en el campeonato de béisbol.

_____ 46. Carlos invitó a Elisa a comer pizza hoy.

_____ 47. Elisa tiene una cita con Pablo el sábado.

_____ 48. Elisa ya tiene planes para mañana.

_____ 49. Elisa no quiere ir al museo porque tiene que estudiar álgebra.

_____ 50. Finalmente Carlos y Elisa deciden ir a un partido de béisbol.

SCORE ____

Nombre _____ Clase _____ Fecha _____

III. Culture

Maximum Score: 15 points

A. Read the following descriptions and indicate whether the person is more likely to be from **a) the United States** or **b) a Spanish-speaking country**. (5 points)

_____ 51. Gloria buys everything in a large supermarket.

_____ 52. Andrea's family eats a very light supper.

_____ 53. Carolina uses **pesos** when shopping.

_____ 54. Daniel drives his car everywhere.

_____ 55. David thinks soccer is more important than football.

SCORE _____

B. Are the following statements **a) true** or **b) false**? (5 points)

_____ 56. Students in Latin American schools only get two weeks of vacation in the summer.

_____ 57. People in Spanish-speaking countries celebrate their saint's day in addition to their birthday.

_____ 58. Some monetary units in Latin America are named after Spanish explorers.

_____ 59. Many girls in Spanish-speaking countries have a big celebration on their fifteenth birthday.

_____ 60. Baseball is the national sport in Spain and in Mexico.

SCORE _____

C. Choose the most appropriate answer to complete each statement below. (5 points)

_____ 61. Families in Spanish-speaking countries often do not have cars because _____.
   a. public transportation is convenient and inexpensive
   b. they are usually more expensive
   c. a and b

_____ 62. Religious and public celebrations in Spanish-speaking countries are often _____.
   a. closely related
   b. very different
   c. none of the above

_____ 63. Many Spanish-speaking baseball players in the U.S. come from _____.
   a. Spain
   b. Chile
   c. Puerto Rico

_____ 64. Spain's **paradores**, or *inns*, are usually _____.
   a. brand new hotels
   b. old castles and convents
   c. new palaces

_____ 65. In Venezuela, you pay your bills with _____.
   a. pesos
   b. bolívares
   c. colones

SCORE _____

¡Ven conmigo! Level 1

Nombre _____ Clase _____ Fecha _____

IV. Writing
Maximum Score: 35 points

A. Imagine that you're studying for a year in a Spanish-speaking country. How would you ask for the following information? Write a complete question for each topic. (10 points)

How would you...?

66. ask your computer science teacher what his name is
    _____

67. ask a new friend where she or he is from
    _____

68. ask a group of schoolmates what they're going to do after class today
    _____

69. ask someone on campus to tell you where the library is
    _____

70. politely ask a bystander what time it is
    _____

SCORE _____

B. You're still living in a Spanish-speaking country. What kind of ordinary questions do you think people would ask you during a typical week? Write a complete sentence to answer each question below. (10 points)

71. ¿Cómo es tu familia?
    _____
    _____

72. ¿Te gusta la comida picante?
    _____
    _____

73. ¿No vas a la fiesta de Chucho mañana? ¿Pero por qué?
    _____
    _____

Nombre _____ Clase _____ Fecha _____

74. ¿Adónde fuiste ayer? Te busqué en casa pero no te encontré.

_____

_____

75. ¿Qué te gustaría hacer para las vacaciones este año? ¿Por qué?

_____

_____

SCORE _____

C. Now that you've been living in Pueblo Nuevo for a while, you know your way around better than most foreigners. Imagine that you're standing at the spot marked with an X. Help the newer visitors by completing the directions to the places they're looking for. (5 points)

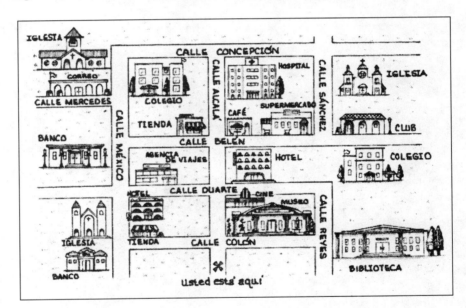

76. ¿La tienda? No, no queda lejos. Está a dos _____ de aquí.

77. Sí, señorita, el correo _____ en la calle Mercedes.

78. Mire, señor, la biblioteca está muy _____ de aquí.

79. Sí, el supermercado está al _____ del Café La Cucharona.

80. Lo siento, señora, creo que no _____ una panadería.

SCORE _____

¡Ven conmigo! Level 1

Nombre _____ Clase _____ Fecha _____

D. Write a paragraph in Spanish describing your dream vacation. Make sure that you include the following elements: where you want to go and why, who you want to go with, and several things you plan to do there. Be creative! (10 points)

81. _____

_____

_____

_____

_____

_____

_____

SCORE ☐

TOTAL SCORE ☐ /100

Nombre _____ Clase _____ Fecha _____

Final Exam Score Sheet

Circle the letter that matches the most appropriate response.

I. Listening
Maximum Score: 30 points

A. (5 points) **B.** (10 points) **C.** (10 points) **D.** (5 points)

1. a b
2. a b
3. a b
4. a b
5. a b

6. a b
7. a b
8. a b
9. a b
10. a b
11. a b
12. a b
13. a b
14. a b
15. a b

16. a b
17. a b
18. a b
19. a b
20. a b
21. a b
22. a b
23. a b
24. a b
25. a b

26. a b c d e
27. a b c d e
28. a b c d e
29. a b c d e
30. a b c d e

SCORE ☐   SCORE ☐   SCORE ☐   SCORE ☐

II. Reading
Maximum Score: 20 points

A. (5 points) **B.** (5 points) **C.** (5 points) **D.** (5 points)

31. a b c d e
32. a b c d e
33. a b c d e
34. a b c d e
35. a b c d e

36. a b c d e
37. a b c d e
38. a b c d e
39. a b c d e
40. a b c d e

41. a b
42. a b
43. a b
44. a b
45. a b

46. a b
47. a b
48. a b
49. a b
50. a b

SCORE ☐   SCORE ☐   SCORE ☐   SCORE ☐

¡Ven conmigo! Level 1   Assessment Guide **57**

Nombre _____ Clase _____ Fecha _____

III. Culture

Maximum Score: 15 points

A. (5 points)

51. a b
52. a b
53. a b
54. a b
55. a b

SCORE ☐

B. (5 points)

56. a b
57. a b
58. a b
59. a b
60. a b

SCORE ☐

C. (5 points)

61. a b c
62. a b c
63. a b c
64. a b c
65. a b c

SCORE ☐

IV. Writing

Maximum Score: 35 points

A. (10 points)

66. _____
67. _____
68. _____
69. _____
70. _____

SCORE ☐

B. (10 points)

71. _____
72. _____
73. _____
74. _____
75. _____

SCORE ☐

Nombre _____ Clase _____ Fecha _____

C. (5 points)

76. _____
77. _____
78. _____
79. _____
80. _____

SCORE [   ]

D. (10 points)

81. _____
_____
_____
_____
_____
_____
_____

SCORE [   ]

TOTAL SCORE [   ] /100

¡Ven conmigo! Level 1

Listening Scripts for Final Exam

I. Listening

A.
JORGE Hola, Marta. ¿Cómo estás?
MARTA Estupendo, ¿y tú?
JORGE Muy bien. Oye, ¿qué piensas hacer durante las vacaciones de verano?
MARTA Pienso viajar a América del Sur con mi familia. Nos gustaría visitar Brasil, Argentina y Chile. ¿Y tú? ¿Qué vas a hacer este verano?
JORGE Me gustaría viajar a Puerto Rico para visitar a mis abuelos, pero no puedo. Tengo que trabajar mucho. Voy a trabajar en el Almacén García. Oye, tú vas a necesitar ropa para tu viaje, ¿no?
MARTA Sí, en América del Sur es invierno ahora y hace mucho frío en Chile y Argentina. Pienso comprar una chaqueta nueva y unas botas de cuero.
JORGE Maravilloso. Hay muchas gangas en el Almacén García y yo te puedo ayudar a encontrar cosas baratas. Pero en Brasil no va hacer mucho frío, ¿verdad?
MARTA No. Además, pienso ir a la playa a tomar el sol y al Amazonas a bajar el río en canoa. A mis padres les gustaría hacer turismo en Rio de Janeiro y a mi hermana le gustaría escalar montañas. Por eso vamos a los Andes en Chile.
JORGE Entonces, ¿también vas a comprar ropa para la playa?
MARTA ¡Claro! Un traje de baño nuevo, unas sandalias y unos lentes de sol.
JORGE Muy bien, Marta. ¿Te gustaría ir al Almacén García con toda tu familia?
MARTA Por supuesto, Jorge. Nos encantan las gangas. Chao.
JORGE Hasta pronto.

B.
6. Tengo que lavarme los dientes antes de comer.
7. ¿Me puede traer una decoración para el almuerzo?
8. ¡Tengo mucha sed! ¿Me puede traer el pan dulce?
9. Quisiera huevos con tocino para el desayuno.
10. ¡Uuy, qué frío! Me gustaría tomar un chocolate caliente.
11. Camarero, ¿me puede traer el menú?
12. ¿Te gustaría un flan para el postre?
13. ¡Tengo mucha hambre! Quisiera un café con leche, por favor.
14. Son dos galletas de propina.
15. ¡Los frijoles están deliciosos!

C.
16. Ayer, los estudiantes del 301 celebraron los quince años de Socorro Martínez. El baile terminó hasta la media noche.
17. Los estudiantes de la clase de deportes van a ir a escalar la Montaña Encantada en el mes de julio.
18. La señorita María Moliner va a ir de vacaciones a España. A partir de mañana, no hay clases de español.
19. Ayer, los Ticos de San José no jugaron al béisbol porque estudiaron para el examen de geografía.
20. Mañana, María Ferreti va a dar una clase de literatura argentina en el Salón 201 a las tres de la tarde.
21. El mes pasado, todos los estudiantes del Centro Unión celebraron el aniversario de su escuela.
22. En mayo, la cafetería de la escuela no va a servir limonadas. Sólo jugos de naranja y de mango.
23. Mañana inician las clases especiales de álgebra del profesor Rodríguez.
24. La semana pasada, los estudiantes de fotografía fueron a la fiesta de aniversario del profesor Cuartoscuro.
25. El domingo pasado, los Huracanes de Barcelona ganaron el partido de fútbol contra los Bombones de Madrid.

D.   **26.** —Son cincuenta dólares.
—¡Cincuenta dólares por un collar! ¡Es un robo!

27. —¡Estas flores rojas son preciosas! ¿Tú crees que le gusten a mamá?
—¡Claro! Estas flores y una tarjeta la van a hacer feliz el Día de las Madres.

28. —¡Qué zapatos tan bonitos! ¡Te quedan muy bien!
—Y además, ¡son muy baratos!

29. —Señorita, ¿me puede decir el precio de este pastel de fresa?
—Lo siento, pero ese pastel es para una fiesta de cumpleaños. ¿Le gustaría un pastel de chocolate?

30. —¡Me encantan los chocolates!
—Pero yo prefiero los dulces.

Answers to Final Exam

I. Listening Maximum Score: 30 points

A. (5 points: 1 point per item)
1. b
2. a
3. a
4. b
5. b

B. (10 points: 1 point per item)
6. b
7. b
8. b
9. a
10. a
11. a
12. a
13. b
14. b
15. a

C. (10 points: 1 point per item)
16. a
17. b
18. b
19. a
20. b
21. a
22. b
23. b
24. a
25. a

D. (5 points: 1 point per item)
26. b
27. c
28. e
29. a
30. d

II. Reading Maximum Score: 20 points

A. (5 points: 1 point per item)
31. d
32. c
33. e
34. a
35. b

B. (5 points: 1 point per item)
36. c
37. a
38. d
39. e
40. b

C. (5 points: 1 point per item)
41. b
42. a
43. a
44. b
45. a

D. (5 points: 1 point per item)
46. a
47. a
48. a
49. a
50. b

III. Culture Maximum Score: 15 points

A. (5 points: 1 point per item)
51. a
52. b
53. b
54. a
55. b

B. (5 points: 1 point per item)
56. b
57. a
58. a
59. a
60. b

C. (5 points: 1 point per item)
61. c
62. a
63. c
64. b
65. b

IV. Writing Maximum Score: 35 points

A. (10 points: 2 point per item)
66. ¿Cómo se llama usted?
67. ¿De dónde eres?
68. ¿Qué van a hacer ustedes hoy después de clase?
69. ¿Me puede(s) decir dónde queda la biblioteca?
70. ¿Qué hora es, por favor?

B. (10 points: 2 point per item) *Possible answers:*
71. Mi familia no es muy grande. Tengo una hermana. Somos una familia unida.
72. No, no me gusta la comida picante.
73. No puedo ir porque tengo mucha tarea.
74. Fui a la doctora porque me siento bastante mal.
75. Me gustaría ir a Colorado porque me encanta escalar montañas y acampar.

C. (5 points: 1 point per item)
76. cuadras
77. queda/está
78. cerca
79. lado
80. hay

D. (10 points) Answers will vary for number 81.